Explore Andalucía and the Costa del Sol on a Budget

Insight-filled Pocket Guide to Unforgettable Experiences Updated For 2024 | Seaside Walks, Moon Views, Mediterranean Golden Beaches, Camping Sites

GREG I. RAMOS

GREG I. RAMOS

Explore Andalucía and the Costa del Sol on a Budget

Outline

Prologue

Exploring Andalucía and the Costa del Sol on a budget was an enchanting adventure that surpassed all expectations. The vibrant culture, stunning landscapes, and warm hospitality made it a truly memorable experience.

Upon arriving in Andalucía, the captivating blend of Moorish architecture and Spanish charm immediately caught my eye. The narrow cobblestone streets of cities like Granada and Seville echoed with the sounds of flamenco music, creating an atmosphere that was both lively and authentic. Despite being on a budget, I discovered that many of the region's most awe-inspiring attractions, including the Alhambra and the Cathedral of Seville, offered affordable or even free entry at certain times.

The journey along the Costa del Sol was equally captivating.

The glistening Mediterranean Sea and golden beaches provided a picturesque backdrop for leisurely strolls. Though luxury resorts dotted the coastline, I found that charming seaside villages like Nerja and Estepona offered budget-friendly accommodations without compromising on the breathtaking views.

One of the highlights of my trip was savoring the local cuisine. From indulging in tapas at bustling marketplaces to relishing fresh seafood in beachside Chiringuitos, every meal was a celebration of Andalusian flavors. The affordability of local eateries allowed me to savor traditional dishes without breaking the bank.

The budget-friendly public transportation system made it easy to explore the region. Buses and trains connected cities and towns, offering a convenient and cost-effective way to discover the diverse landscapes of Andalucía.

Venturing into the scenic countryside, I marveled at olive groves, vineyards, and whitewashed villages perched on hillsides.

As the sun dipped below the horizon, I couldn't resist joining the locals for a lively evening on the streets. Whether it was participating in a spontaneous flamenco performance or sipping on affordable local wines, the energy of Andalucía's nightlife was contagious.

In the end, my budget-friendly journey through Andalucía and the Costa del Sol was a testament to the notion that the best experiences often lie beyond the confines of luxury. The warmth of the people, the richness of the culture, and the sheer beauty of the surroundings left an indelible mark on my heart, making it a truly beautiful and unforgettable adventure.

Overview

(Setting the tone for a budget-friendly adventure)

Embarking on a budget-friendly adventure through the enchanting landscapes of Andalucía and the sun-kissed shores of the Costa del Sol promises a journey unlike any other. Nestled in the southern part of Spain, this region is a treasure trove of Moorish architecture, lively traditions, and breathtaking scenery. Our guide invites you to explore the rich Canvas of Andalusian culture and the allure of the coastal haven, all while embracing the art of savvy travel.

As we delve into the heart of Andalucía, imagine wandering through narrow cobblestone streets resonating with the soul-stirring notes of flamenco music. Picture the iconic Alhambra and the Cathedral of Seville, where budget-friendly exploration unveils the historical grandeur that defines the region.

Join us in discovering the warmth of the people, the richness of the culture, and the affordability of a destination that beckons with open arms.

Venturing along the Costa del Sol, we'll guide you to charming seaside villages that offer not only a respite for the budget-conscious traveler but also panoramic views of the Mediterranean that defy description. Imagine relishing the flavors of Andalusian cuisine without breaking the bank, indulging in tapas at lively markets, and savoring fresh seafood in beachside Chiringuitos.

Throughout this guide, we'll share insights on budget-friendly accommodations, transportation tips, and the best-kept secrets of Andalucía and the Costa del Sol. So, buckle up for an adventure where affordability meets unparalleled beauty, and every twist and turn reveals the magic of a region that invites exploration without compromise. Welcome to a budget-friendly escapade through the heart and soul of southern Spain.

Pre-Trip Planning: Unlocking Affordable Adventures

Embarking on a budget-friendly journey through Andalucía and the Costa del Sol requires a strategic approach to pre-trip planning. By mastering the art of frugal exploration, you can stretch your travel budget without sacrificing the essence of the experience.

1.Researching Budget Accommodations:

Begin your adventure by securing wallet-friendly accommodations that don't compromise on comfort or authenticity. Delve into the myriad of options, from charming guest houses in historic city centers to budget-friendly beachfront hostels along the Costa del Sol. Online platforms, local travel forums, and booking websites often unveil hidden gems that cater to the budget-conscious traveler. Look for accommodations that offer a genuine taste of local life, ensuring a more immersive and economical stay.

2. Finding Affordable Transportation Options:

Navigate the expansive landscapes of Andalucía without breaking the bank by exploring budget-friendly transportation alternatives. Embrace the extensive network of buses and trains that connect cities and towns, providing an affordable and picturesque means of travel. Research regional travel passes or discount cards that offer significant savings on transportation costs. By choosing cost-effective options, you not only minimize expenses but also gain a more authentic perspective of the diverse terrain.

3. Identifying Budget-Friendly Activities and Attractions:

Uncover the wealth of budget-friendly activities and attractions that Andalucía and the Costa del Sol generously offer.

Take advantage of free entry days or discounted admission to iconic sites such as the Alhambra or the Cathedral of Seville. Immerse yourself in the vibrant street life of local markets, where the essence of Andalusian culture unfolds without a price tag. Seek out lesser-known gems, from hidden hiking trails to tranquil beaches, providing memorable experiences without straining your budget.

Armed with these pre-trip planning strategies, you'll not only embark on a journey that respects your budget but also unlock the true essence of Andalucía and the Costa del Sol. Prepare for an adventure where every penny saved contributes to a richer, more fulfilling travel experience.

Arrival in Andalucía: Unveiling Timeless Charms

Stepping onto the sun-drenched soil of Andalucía, one is immediately captivated by the region's unique charm—a mesmerizing blend of Moorish heritage, vibrant traditions, and warm hospitality. As you begin your journey, the air is infused with the scent of orange blossoms, and the streets echo with the lively rhythms of flamenco, setting the stage for an unforgettable experience.

First Impressions of the Region's Unique Charm:

Wander through the narrow cobblestone streets of cities like Granada and Seville, where whitewashed buildings adorned with wrought-iron balconies transport you to a bygone era. Take in the grandeur of historic landmarks, each bearing the indelible mark of Andalusian history.

The architectural marvels, such as the Alcazar and the Giralda Tower, stand as testaments to a rich and diverse cultural heritage.

Immerse yourself in the vibrant street life, where locals engage in animated conversations at bustling markets and lively plazas. The warmth of the people and the authenticity of their daily rituals create an atmosphere that is both inviting and intoxicating.

Budget-Friendly Entry to Iconic Attractions:

Despite the grandeur of Andalucía's iconic attractions, budget-friendly access is within reach. The Alhambra, a UNESCO World Heritage Site and a pinnacle of Moorish architecture, opens its doors for free entry on certain days and times. Planning your visit accordingly allows you to marvel at the intricate details of the Nasrid Palaces and the Generalife Gardens without straining your budget.

In Seville, the Cathedral, with its Gothic architecture and the famous La Giralda tower, offers budget-conscious travelers the opportunity to explore for free during specific hours. Ascend to the tower for panoramic views of the city, capturing the essence of Seville without breaking the bank.

Prepare to be enchanted as you navigate the labyrinthine streets and unveil the hidden treasures that Andalucía holds. From the first glimpse to the exploration of iconic landmarks, the region welcomes budget travelers with open arms, ensuring that every moment is an immersion into the unique and timeless charm of southern Spain.

Exploring Andalusian Cities

(A Canvas of History, Culture, and Affordability)

Venturing into the heart of Andalucía means traversing a landscape adorned with cities steeped in history, where the echoes of Moorish wonders and the pulse of Andalusian culture resonate through the cobbled streets. In this journey, we'll immerse ourselves in the budget-friendly allure of Granada and Seville, unraveling the stories etched in their walls. Additionally, we'll provide invaluable local tips to navigate the enchanting cities of Cordoba, Malaga, and beyond.

Granada: A City of Moorish Wonders on a Budget

Granada, nestled at the foothills of the Sierra Nevada mountains, is a testament to the rich Moorish legacy that shaped Andalusia.

The crown jewel of Granada is undoubtedly the Alhambra, a fortress complex that encapsulates the opulence and sophistication of Moorish art and architecture. To experience this marvel on a budget, plan your visit during the designated free entry hours or explore the surrounding areas, such as the Albaicín neighborhood, which offers stunning views of the Alhambra without the cost.

As you navigate the labyrinthine streets of the Albaicín, you'll encounter whitewashed houses adorned with colorful tiles and hidden squares where locals gather. The Mirador de San Nicolás provides an iconic panorama of the Alhambra against the backdrop of the Sierra Nevada—a postcard-worthy view without spending a dime.

Delve into the vibrant fabric of Granada's street life at the Alcaicería, the city's historic bazaar. Here, you can haggle for spices, textiles, and souvenirs, immersing yourself in the lively atmosphere of an ancient Moorish market.

Enjoy a budget-friendly meal at a local tetería (tea house), where the scent of exotic teas and the strains of flamenco music transport you to the heart of Andalusian culture.

Seville: Discovering the Heart of Andalucía Affordably

Seville, the beating heart of Andalucía, beckons with its captivating blend of Gothic and Moorish architecture, lively neighborhoods, and iconic landmarks. Begin your exploration at the Plaza de España, a grand square adorned with bridges, canals, and a sweeping semicircular building representing the epitome of Spanish Renaissance Revival style. Entry is free, allowing you to bask in the grandeur of this architectural masterpiece without denting your budget.

Adjacent to the Plaza de España stands the Maria Luisa Park, a sprawling green oasis dotted with fountains, statues, and quiet corners.

Stroll beneath the shade of towering palm trees, reveling in the serenity of this public park that offers an escape from the bustling city.

The Seville Cathedral, a UNESCO World Heritage Site, invites budget-conscious travelers to marvel at its awe-inspiring interior for free during specific hours. Climb La Giralda, the cathedral's bell tower, for panoramic views of Seville's skyline and the Guadalquivir River, capturing the essence of the city from above.

Navigate the historic Barrio Santa Cruz, Seville's former Jewish quarter, where narrow alleys lead to hidden plazas adorned with orange trees. Lose yourself in the enchanting labyrinth, stumbling upon charming cafes and boutiques that embody the local spirit.

Local Tips for Navigating Cordoba, Malaga, and Beyond

Cordoba: A Fusion of Cultures in the Heart of Andalucía

Cordoba, with its captivating blend of Islamic, Christian, and Jewish influences, stands as a living testament to the coexistence of cultures throughout history. The crown jewel of Cordoba is the Mezquita, a mosque-cathedral that encapsulates the city's rich cultural tapestry. Plan your visit during the designated free hours to witness the interplay of light and shadow within this architectural marvel.

Wander through the narrow streets of the Judería, Cordoba's Jewish quarter, where whitewashed buildings adorned with colorful flowers create a picturesque setting. The Calleja de las Flores, a narrow alleyway bursting with floral displays, leads to the Plaza del Potro, a charming square surrounded by cafes and artisan workshops.

Cross the Roman Bridge spanning the Guadalquivir River to reach the Torre de la Calahorra, a fortress that houses the Museum of Al-Andalus Life. Explore the exhibits detailing the history of Islamic Cordoba, providing insights into the city's golden age.

Malaga: The Coastal Gem with Artistic Allure

Malaga, often overshadowed by its coastal charm, boasts a rich cultural heritage and a burgeoning art scene. Begin your exploration at the Alcazaba, a medieval fortress with sprawling gardens that offer panoramic views of the city and the Mediterranean Sea. Entry is budget-friendly, making it an ideal starting point for your Malaga adventure.

Stroll through the historic center, where the Malaga Cathedral and the Picasso Museum beckon art enthusiasts.

To appreciate Picasso's genius without the cost, visit the museum during its free evening hours on Sundays.

Malaga's beachfront, Playa de la Malagueta, invites relaxation with its golden sands and vibrant promenade. Join locals for an evening paseo (stroll) along the waterfront, savoring the sea breeze and the view of the city bathed in the warm glow of sunset.

Local Tips for Exploring Andalusian Cities:

- Use Public Transportation: In cities like Granada, Seville, and Malaga, utilize cost-effective public transportation options, including buses and trams, to navigate the urban landscape. This not only saves money but also provides a local experience.

- Dine Like a Local: Venture away from tourist hotspots to discover authentic and budget-friendly eateries. Look for tapas bars serving small, affordable dishes, and explore neighborhood markets for fresh, local ingredients.

- Free Walk Tours: Many cities give free walk tours led by Experienced locals. Joining these tours provides insights into the history, culture, and hidden gems of each city without breaking your budget.

- Explore Off-Peak Hours: Visit popular attractions during off-peak hours or on designated free days to maximize your budget. Planning your itinerary strategically allows you to experience iconic landmarks without the crowds.

- Stay in Locally-Owned Accommodations: Opt for budget-friendly accommodations that are locally owned, such as guesthouses and boutique hotels.

Not only does this support the local economy, but it also provides a more personalized experience.

As you navigate the diverse cities of Andalucía, each unveiling its unique history and cultural canvas, remember that the true essence of the region lies not only in its iconic landmarks but also in the everyday life of its streets, squares, and neighborhoods. Allow the rhythm of Flamenco, the scent of orange blossoms, and the warmth of the locals to guide your exploration, creating memories that transcend the confines of a budget.

Affordable Accommodations with Stunning Coastal Views

As the sun dips below the horizon along the Costa del Sol, your heaven awaits—affordable accommodations that not only promise comfort but also boast unparallele views of the Mediterranean. Prepare to be enchanted as we explore boutique stays, seaside hostels, and coastal camping options that have been carefully chosen for their unique charm, a touch of history, and budget-friendly allure.

1. Seaside Hostels and Guesthouses:

Albergue Playamar, Nerja
This guest house is Located just 1 km away from the coast
(+34) 952 529 582
playamaro@hotelplayamaro.com

Situated in the heart of Nerja, the Albergue Playamar effortlessly blends affordability with an authentic Andalusian atmosphere.

Originally established as a coastal retreat for fishermen, this charming hostel has evolved into a haven for budget-conscious travelers seeking proximity to the sea.

The Albergue Playamar, with its whitewashed facade and azure accents, exudes a maritime charm that mirrors Nerja's coastal identity. The hotel's terrace, adorned with colorful bougainvillea, offers stunning views of the Mediterranean, creating an ideal spot to unwind after a day of exploration.

Affordability Meter:
£58 per night

Alternate Choice: Hostal Marissal, Nerja

Nestled along Nerja's picturesque coastline, Hostal Marissal embodies a blend of affordability and coastal charm.

Originally a family home, this guesthouse retains its Andalusian character while providing a warm and welcoming atmosphere. The rooms, adorned with traditional decor, offer glimpses of the Mediterranean, and the communal terrace invites you to unwind as you soak in the sea views.

Affordability Meter:

Double rooms: €42.70 to £89.50 per night

2. Boutique Stays with Local Flavor:

Harmony of Past and Present: Hotel Buenavista, Estepona

Located at Paseo Maritimo, 180, 29680 Estepona Spain

+34 95 280 01 37

Nestled in Estepona's Old Town, the Hotel Buenavista seamlessly integrates modern comforts with the town's historical backdrop.

Originally a traditional Andalusian residence, this boutique hotel showcases architectural elements from its past while providing affordable elegance for the modern traveler.

Each room at Hotel Buenavista offers a unique blend of rustic charm and contemporary amenities, creating an intimate retreat. The hotel's rooftop terrace, overlooking Estepona's rooftops and the sea, invites you to savor the panoramic views—a testament to the property's commitment to capturing the essence of the coastal experience.

Affordability Meter:

Standard double room: €60-80 per night

Alternate Choice: Hotel Casa Veracruz, Estepona

Address at C. Veracruz, 22, 29680 Estepona, Málaga, Spain
+34 674 95 47 77

Hotel Casa Veracruz, located in Estepona's historic heart, offers an alternative boutique experience. This hotel, once a grand residence, has been meticulously restored to showcase its original architectural splendor. The individually designed rooms provide a harmonious blend of historic elegance and contemporary comfort. The courtyard, adorned with fragrant orange trees, serves as a tranquil oasis where you can enjoy the sea breeze.

Affordability Meter:

Double rooms: €70-90 per night

3. Camping by the Sea:

Under the Stars: Camping Playa de Poniente, Almuñécar

For the adventurer seeking a closer connection to nature, Camping Playa de Poniente in Almuñécar provides a seaside camping experience with budget-friendly rates.

Originally a family-owned campsite, it has evolved into a tranquil retreat where the sound of waves lulls you to sleep beneath the starlit Costa del Sol sky.

Camping Playa de Poniente, nestled between the beach and the mountains, offers a unique opportunity to wake up to the gentle murmur of the Mediterranean. Whether you choose a tent pitch or a caravan spot, each night becomes a seaside sojourn, allowing you to revel in the simplicity of coastal camping.

Affordability Meter:

Tent pitch: €15-20 per night
Caravan spot: €20-25 per night

Alternate Choice: Camping La Herradura, La Herradura

For a coastal camping alternative, consider Camping La Herradura, situated in the bay of La Herradura. This family-friendly campsite offers a serene environment, surrounded by lush greenery and just steps away from the beach.

The shaded pitches and proximity to the historic town make it an excellent choice for those seeking a balance between nature and culture.

Affordability Meter:

Tent pitch: €20-25 per night
Caravan spot: €25-30 per night

Why We Chose Them for You:

- Albergue Playamar, Nerja: Its history as a fisherman's retreat, combined with unbeatable affordability and stunning coastal views from the terrace, makes it a quintessential Nerja experience.

- Hotel Buenavista, Estepona: The blend of traditional Andalusian architecture and modern comfort, coupled with a rooftop terrace offering panoramic views, provides a unique and memorable stay in Estepona's historic center.

- Camping Playa de Poniente, Almuñécar: For those craving an intimate connection with nature, this family-owned campsite allows you to camp by the sea, offering a budget-friendly and unforgettably scenic experience.

Whether you choose the communal spirit of a seaside hostel, the boutique elegance of a historic hotel, or the simplicity of coastal camping, each option beckons with its own allure, promising affordability without compromising the breathtaking coastal vistas that define the Costa del Sol. The choice is yours—to wake up to the sound of the waves and the warmth of the Andalusian sun, creating memories that linger far beyond the journey's end.

Costa del Sol Adventures

Budget-Friendly Seaside Villages

As you embark on the exploration of budget-friendly seaside villages along the sun-kissed Costa del Sol, prepare to be captivated by the unique allure of each destination. We'll take a stroll through Nerja, Estepona, and other hidden gems, uncovering the picturesque landscapes, vibrant culture, and affordability that make these coastal havens truly unforgettable.

1. Explore the Charm of Nerja:

As the sun casts its golden hues over the Mediterranean, the town of Nerja emerges as a radiant gem along the coastline. Begin your journey at the iconic Balcony of Europe, a panoramic promenade perched high above the sea. The azure waters stretch endlessly before you, framed by the rugged cliffs that define the Costa del Sol.

Descend into the heart of Nerja's historic center, where narrow cobblestone streets wind through whitewashed buildings adorned with vibrant bougainvillea. The scent of saltwater mingles with the aromas of local cuisine as charming cafes beckon with promises of authentic Andalusian flavors.

Pause at the Church of El Salvador, a centuries-old structure that stands as a testament to Nerja's rich history. Its rustic facade and serene atmosphere invite contemplation before you continue your journey through the labyrinthine alleys.

Discover hidden corners like Plaza Cavana, a bustling square where locals converge for lively conversations. The rhythmic beats of flamenco music may guide you to intimate venues, where spontaneous performances unfold, creating an immersive experience in the heart of Nerja's cultural tapestry.

2. Estepona's Tranquil Beauty:

Transitioning to Estepona, you find yourself in a haven of tranquility where time seems to slow down. The Old Town welcomes you with flower-filled streets, charming squares, and colorful murals that adorn the facades of buildings. Each step through Estepona's historic quarter unveils a mural-painted surprise, offering a unique blend of art and history.

Make your way to Plaza de las Flores, a central square where locals and visitors alike gather to savor the ambiance. Sidewalk cafes spill into the plaza, offering an ideal spot to indulge in a leisurely coffee while absorbing the Mediterranean vibes.

Estepona's beaches, like Playa del Cristo, beckon with their golden sands and crystal-clear waters. Nestled in a sheltered cove, Playa del Cristo provides a serene escape where the gentle lapping of waves creates a soothing soundtrack to your coastal retreat.

As evening descends, stroll along the Paseo Marítimo, Estepona's seaside promenade. Illuminated by the glow of streetlights and the distant twinkle of fishing boats, the promenade offers a tranquil setting for a moonlit walk, providing a perfect conclusion to your day in Estepona.

3. Beyond the Classics: Explore Hidden Gems:

Venture off the beaten path to discover the lesser-known treasures that dot the Costa del Sol. Explore Almuñécar, where the Playa Puerta del Mar unfolds its tranquil beauty, offering a respite from the busier beaches. The historic Old Town, with its narrow alleys and charming squares, invites exploration, providing a glimpse into the authentic Andalusian lifestyle.

In Mijas, a mountain village overlooking the Mediterranean, the traditional white-washed architecture contrasts against the azure sky.

The Plaza de la Constitución, adorned with colorful flowerpots, becomes a visual feast, inviting you to sit and soak in the ambiance of this hidden gem.

These villages, often overshadowed by their more famous counterparts, offer a unique and budget-friendly escape. Delve into their local markets, engage with friendly residents, and witness the untouched beauty that defines the Costa del Sol beyond the classics.

As you tread the coastal paths of Nerja, Estepona, and these hidden gems, each step becomes a brushstroke on the canvas of your Andalusian adventure. The memories of charming streets, panoramic vistas, and the warmth of the Mediterranean sun will linger, creating an indelible imprint of the budget-friendly seaside villages that grace the Costa del Sol.

Exploring Nerja, Estepona, and Other Hidden Gems: A Coastal Odyssey

As the sun-drenched coastline of the Costa del Sol beckons, we embark on a captivating journey through Nerja, Estepona, and the lesser-known treasures that lie off the beaten path. Each step unveils an array of history, culture, and breathtaking vistas, creating an indelible memory of Andalusia's coastal charms.

Nerja: Balcony of the Mediterranean

Balcon de Europa:

Our journey begins in Nerja, where the Balcon de Europa stands as the crowning jewel, offering an unparalleled panoramic view of the Mediterranean.

As you stand on the Balcony of Europe, perched high above the sea, the azure expanse stretches infinitely, framed by the rugged cliffs that define the Costa del Sol.

History:
Originally a fortress built by the Moors, the Balcon de Europa gained its current name in the mid-20th century when King Alfonso XII visited and declared it the "Balcony of Europe." The fortress, strategically positioned for defense, has transformed into a breathtaking promenade that serves as the perfect introduction to Nerja.

Fun Fact:
The Balcon de Europa serves as the setting for various cultural events, including concerts and festivals, providing a unique blend of scenic beauty and artistic expression.

Stroll through the Old Town:

Descending from the Balcon de Europa, you find yourself in the heart of Nerja's historic Old Town.

Cobblestone streets wind through whitewashed buildings adorned with vibrant bougainvillea, creating a charming backdrop for your exploration.

History:
The Old Town, with its narrow alleys and traditional architecture, reflects Nerja's Moorish and Mediterranean heritage. Many buildings date back to the 17th century, offering a tangible link to the town's rich history.

Fun Fact:
Calle Carabeo, one of the oldest streets in Nerja, is lined with traditional houses and leads to hidden coves, inviting you to discover the town's authentic charm.

Church of El Salvador:

As you wander deeper into the Old Town, the Church of El Salvador emerges—a centuries-old structure that stands as a testament to Nerja's spiritual heritage. The rustic facade and serene atmosphere invite contemplation.

History:
Built in the 17th century, the Church of El Salvador combines Gothic and Baroque elements, representing the religious fervor that shaped Nerja's architecture during this period.

Fun Fact:
The church's interior houses a collection of religious art, including paintings and sculptures that offer insights into Nerja's artistic heritage.

Plaza Cavana:

Navigating the Old Town, you stumble upon Plaza Cavana, a bustling square where locals and visitors converge for lively conversations. The rhythmic beats of flamenco music may guide you to intimate venues, where spontaneous performances unfold.

History:
Plaza Cavana has been a central gathering place for centuries, hosting markets, festivals, and social events.

The lively atmosphere captures the essence of Nerja's vibrant community life.

Fun Fact:
Cavana is named after the Arabic word "Kahwana," meaning coffee, reflecting the square's historical connection to the town's coffee culture.

Estepona: A Tranquil Haven in Andalusia

Estepona's Old Town:

Transitioning to Estepona, a haven of tranquility unfolds where time seems to slow down. The Old Town, with its flower-filled streets and vibrant murals, invites exploration. Each step through Estepona's historic quarter unveils a mural-painted surprise, offering a unique blend of art and history.

History:
Estepona's Old Town dates back to the 16th century when it was established as a fishing and agricultural village.

The narrow streets and whitewashed houses reflect the town's Moorish origins and its subsequent evolution under Christian rule.

Fun Fact:
Estepona's mural project, initiated in 2012, has transformed the town into an open-air art gallery, with over 60 murals depicting various themes, from maritime scenes to cultural symbols.

Plaza de las Flores:

Make your way to Plaza de las Flores, a central square where locals and visitors alike gather to savor the ambiance. Sidewalk cafes spill into the plaza, offering an ideal spot to indulge in a leisurely coffee while absorbing the Mediterranean vibes.

History:
Plaza de las Flores has been Estepona's social hub for centuries, hosting markets, celebrations, and community gatherings.

The colorful flowerpots that adorn the square create a vibrant and welcoming atmosphere.

Fun Fact:
The square's central fountain, named Fuente de las Flores, is adorned with ceramic tiles and serves as a focal point for the town's annual celebrations.

Playa del Cristo:

Estepona's beaches, like Playa del Cristo, beckon with their golden sands and crystal-clear waters. Nestled in a sheltered cove, Playa del Cristo provides a serene escape where the gentle lapping of waves creates a soothing soundtrack to your coastal retreat.

History:
Playa del Cristo's name translates to "Christ's Beach," with locals believing that the statue of Christ, now housed in the Church of El Salvador, once washed ashore here.

Fun Fact:
The beach is renowned for its shallow and calm waters, making it an ideal spot for families and those seeking a relaxed seaside experience.

Paseo Marítimo:

As evening descends, stroll along the Paseo Marítimo, Estepona's seaside promenade. Illuminated by the glow of streetlights and the distant twinkle of fishing boats, the promenade offers a tranquil setting for a moonlit walk, providing a perfect conclusion to your day in Estepona.

History:
The Paseo Marítimo was developed in the 1980s as part of Estepona's commitment to enhancing its coastal offerings. It has since become a beloved space for leisurely walks and enjoying the sea breeze.

Fun Fact:
Estepona's Paseo Marítimo hosts a vibrant Sunday market, where locals and tourists

alike gather to browse through artisanal crafts, jewelry, and local produce.

Hidden Gems: Beyond the Classics

Almuñécar:

Venture off the beaten path to discover Almuñécar, where Playa Puerta del Mar unfolds its tranquil beauty, offering a respite from the busier beaches. The historic Old Town, with its narrow alleys and charming squares, invites exploration, providing a glimpse into the authentic Andalusian lifestyle.

History:
Almuñécar traces its roots back to Phoenician and Roman times, and its historic center is dotted with remnants of these ancient civilizations, including the Roman aqueduct and fish salting factory.

Fun Fact:
The San Miguel Castle, perched on a hilltop, offers panoramic views of Almuñécar and the surrounding coastline,

providing a glimpse into the town's strategic significance throughout history.

Mijas:

In Mijas, a mountain village overlooking the Mediterranean, the traditional white-washed architecture contrasts against the azure sky. The Plaza de la Constitución, adorned with colorful flowerpots, becomes a visual feast, inviting you to sit and soak in the ambiance of this hidden gem.

History:
Mijas dates back to prehistoric times, and its name is derived from the Arabic word "Mihas," meaning "water spring." The village's layout and architecture bear the influence of both Moorish and Andalusian styles.

Fun Fact:
Mijas is home to the Museo Histórico-Etnológico, a museum that showcases the town's history and traditions

through exhibits on agriculture, crafts, and everyday life.

As you traverse the coastal paths of Nerja, Estepona, Almuñécar, Mijas, and other hidden gems, each moment becomes a brushstroke on the canvas of your Andalusian odyssey. The memories of charming streets, panoramic vistas, and the warmth of the Mediterranean sun will linger, creating an indelible imprint of the coastal treasures that grace the Costa del Sol.

Culinary Delights

Sampling Andalusian Cuisine

A Gastronomic Journey on a Budget

Embarking on a culinary adventure through Andalusia is a sensory delight that unfolds with each delectable bite, and the best part? It doesn't have to break the bank. As you traverse the diverse landscapes of this southern Spanish region, be prepared to savor the unique flavors of Andalusian cuisine, a melting pot of influences that has evolved over centuries.

1. Gazpacho: A Chilled Symphony of Tomatoes and Freshness

In the heat of Andalusia, there's no better way to start your gastronomic journey than with a refreshing bowl of gazpacho.

This chilled tomato soup, infused with peppers, onions, garlic, and cucumbers, is a burst of Mediterranean flavors. Originating from the Andalusian countryside, gazpacho was traditionally consumed by field laborers seeking respite from the sun. Today, it's a staple on local menus, offering a cool and budget-friendly respite for travelers exploring the culinary landscape.

2. Salmorejo: A Creamy Tomato Elixir with a Breaded Twist

Venture a bit deeper into Andalusian gastronomy, and you'll encounter salmorejo, a dish that elevates simplicity to an art form. This creamy tomato soup, enriched with olive oil and thickened with bread, has its roots in the region's Moorish past. Originally a humble peasant dish, salmorejo has evolved into a culinary masterpiece, often garnished with hard-boiled eggs and Jamón (cured ham). Indulge in this velvety creation at local eateries, where it's not only a culinary delight but also friendly to your travel budget.

3. Espetos de Sardinas: Skewered Delights from the Mediterranean

As you meander along the coastal towns, the aroma of grilled sardines will inevitably beckon you. Espetos de Sardinas, or skewered sardines, are a seaside specialty that captures the essence of Andalusia's maritime heritage. Dating back to the Phoenician era, this dish is a testament to the region's enduring love affair with the sea. Picture yourself on the beach, where local Chiringuitos (beach bars) offer these skewers fresh off the grill, providing a budget-friendly taste of the Mediterranean.

4. Flamenquín: Andalusian Comfort Food Wrapped in Crispy Goodness

For those seeking comfort on a plate, the flamenquín is a culinary masterpiece that seamlessly marries the best of Andalusian ingredients. Originating in the province of Córdoba, this dish features ham-wrapped pork or chicken, coated in breadcrumbs and deep-fried to golden perfection.

The result is a crispy exterior that gives way to succulent, flavorful meat. Enjoy this hearty dish at local taverns, where it embodies the warmth and hospitality of Andalusian home cooking at a wallet-friendly price.

5. Migas: Savoring the Simplicity of Andalusian Comfort

Migas, a dish born out of resourcefulness, is a testament to Andalusia's agricultural roots. Originally crafted by shepherds using leftover bread, this savory dish has evolved into a beloved comfort food. Imagine a plate of migas adorned with garlic, chorizo, and sometimes grapes, providing a symphony of textures and flavors. Head to rustic taverns and family-run establishments to savor this humble yet satisfying creation without straining your budget.

Navigating Tapas Culture Without Overspending

In the heart of Andalusia, the tapas culture is more than a culinary tradition—it's a vibrant social experience that invites you to savor bite-sized delights while immersed in the lively atmosphere of local bars and eateries. Navigating this culinary landscape without overspending requires a blend of strategy and adventurous spirit. Prepare for a taste bud journey where every tapa becomes a budget-friendly adventure.

1. Embrace the Art of "Tapeo" with Local Insights

To navigate tapas culture successfully, embrace the art of "tapeo"—the practice of hopping from one tapas bar to another. Consult locals for their favorite spots, as they often hold the keys to hidden gems that offer generous portions without hefty price tags.

Engage in conversation with bartenders and fellow patrons; you might find yourself discovering the next must-try tapa.

2. Seek Out Traditional Taverns and Local Favorites

While tourist hotspots may lure you with flashy presentations, the true essence of tapas culture is often found in traditional taverns frequented by locals. These establishments, adorned with aged barrels and authentic charm, offer a more intimate and budget-friendly experience. Opt for local favorites like boquerones (anchovies), patatas bravas (spicy potatoes), and albóndigas (meatballs) for an authentic taste of Andalusia without breaking the bank.

3. Embrace the "Free Tapas" Tradition in Some Regions

In certain regions of Andalusia, particularly Granada, the tradition of complimentary tapas with your drink still thrives.

Take advantage of this budget-friendly practice, where ordering a beverage often comes with a delightful surprise of a free tapa. Explore the diverse offerings as you sip your drink, and let the rhythm of the local tapas scene unfold without worrying about the bill.

4. Opt for "Raciones" for Shared Affordability

While the allure of individual tapas is undeniable, consider ordering "raciones" for shared affordability. Raciones are larger portions meant for sharing among friends, allowing you to explore a variety of flavors without accumulating a hefty tab. This communal approach not only fosters a convivial atmosphere but also offers a practical way to navigate tapas culture without overspending.

5. Time Your Tapas Adventure Strategically

Timing is key when navigating tapas culture on a budget.

Many bars offer special tapas deals during specific hours, often referred to as "happy hour." Plan your tapas adventure during these times to take advantage of discounted prices and promotions. Whether it's an early evening stroll or a late-night exploration, strategic timing allows you to savor the best of tapas culture without straining your budget.

6. Explore Tapas Routes for Budget-Friendly Variety

Tapas routes, known as "Rutas de Tapas," are organized events where participating bars showcase their best offerings at a fixed, budget-friendly price. These routes provide an excellent opportunity to sample diverse tapas without overspending. Check local event calendars or inquire with your accommodation for information on ongoing tapas routes during your visit.

Best Budget-Friendly Local Eateries

In the labyrinth of Andalusian streets, where the scent of olive oil mingles with the warmth of Mediterranean spices, discovering the best budget-friendly local eateries is like uncovering hidden treasures. These establishments, often cherished by locals, promise an authentic gastronomic experience without putting a dent in your wallet. Let the culinary exploration begin as we unveil the gems of Andalusia's dining scene.

1. Bar Los Diamantes, Granada: A Tapas Institution

Nestled in the heart of Granada, Bar Los Diamantes stands as an institution in the world of tapas. Renowned for its fresh seafood offerings, this unassuming bar lures locals and savvy travelers alike. Order a drink, and watch as a complimentary tapa arrives—a tradition that adds to the allure of Los Diamantes.

From fried fish to seafood paella, this budget-friendly gem offers a taste of the Mediterranean without compromising quality.

2. Bodegas Castañeda, Granada: Where Tradition Meets Affordability

In the historic Albayzín district of Granada, Bodegas Castañeda beckons with its historic charm and pocket-friendly tapas. Step into this quintessential Andalusian tavern, where the walls are adorned with bullfighting memorabilia and the atmosphere hums with conviviality. Sip on local wines and indulge in an array of tapas, from chorizo to olives, as you immerse yourself in the rich traditions of Granada's culinary scene.

3. Casa Morales, Seville: Tantalizing Taste Buds on a Budget

Seville, with its lively ambiance and vibrant food culture, is home to Casa Morales, a centuries-old tavern that seamlessly blends history with affordability.

As you step into the tiled interior, the aroma of Spanish spices fills the air. Casa Morales is renowned for its montaditos—small sandwiches bursting with flavor. Order a selection, pair them with a glass of local wine, and savor the authentic tastes of Seville without breaking the bank.

4. Taberna Coloniales, Seville: A Tapas Haven in the Heart of the City

Situated near Seville's iconic Cathedral, Taberna Coloniales offers a budget-friendly escape into the world of tapas. The outdoor seating provides a perfect vantage point for people-watching while you sample an array of savory treats. From Iberian ham to salmorejo, Taberna Coloniales ensures that each tapa is a testament to Seville's culinary prowess, all within a budget-friendly framework.

5. Casa Puga, Almería: Historic Elegance Meets Affordability

Almería's Casa Puga stands as a testament to the city's Moorish heritage and its culinary traditions. Established in 1870, this historic bar exudes elegance with its tiled walls and vintage décor. Despite its timeless charm, Casa Puga remains a haven for budget-conscious diners. Indulge in regional specialties like espetos de sardinas (grilled sardines) and tapenade-topped montaditos, all served with a side of Almería's warm hospitality.

6. Bodeguita El Gallo, Cordoba: Flavors of Tradition at a Modest Price

Cordoba's Bodeguita El Gallo invites you to step back in time and relish the flavors of Andalusian tradition. This family-run establishment, adorned with bullfighting memorabilia, serves up budget-friendly tapas that reflect the essence of Cordoba's culinary heritage.

From salmorejo to flamenquín, each dish is crafted with care, ensuring that your culinary journey through Cordoba is both satisfying and economical.

7. Mesón Antonio, Malaga: Where Local Flavor Meets Affordability

In the heart of Malaga, Mesón Antonio stands as a testament to the city's dedication to traditional cuisine. This budget-friendly gem welcomes you with its unpretentious charm and a menu brimming with local delights. From albondigas (meatballs) to boquerones (anchovies), Mesón Antonio captures the essence of Malaga's culinary heritage, allowing you to indulge without straining your travel budget.

As you weave through the narrow streets of Granada, Seville, Almería, Cordoba, and Malaga, let these budget-friendly local eateries be your culinary compass.

Each bite is not just a gastronomic experience but a journey into the heart of Andalusian flavors—where affordability meets authenticity, creating memories that linger long after the last tapa is savored.

Budget-Friendly Transportation in Andalusia

Exploring the diverse landscapes of Andalusia doesn't have to strain your budget. With a strategic approach to public transportation and some insider tips for venturing into the countryside, you can traverse this captivating region efficiently without breaking the bank.

1. Cost-Effective Public Transportation in Cities:

Locating Affordable Options:

Buses: Andalusian cities boast well-connected bus networks, providing a cost-effective way to navigate urban landscapes. Look for central bus stations and explore route maps, making note of major landmarks and attractions.

Metro and Trams: In cities like Seville and Malaga, efficient metro and tram systems offer affordable transportation options. Maps are usually available at stations, and tickets can be purchased on-site or through mobile apps.
Cost Ranges:

Bus Tickets: Intra-city bus fares typically range from €1.20 to €1.50 per ride, making it an economical choice for short distances.
Metro/Tram Tickets: Prices for metro and tram rides range from €1.35 to €1.80 per journey, providing a convenient and budget-friendly means of city transportation.

2. Tips for Exploring the Countryside Affordably:

Utilizing Regional Trains:

Locating Train Stations: Regional train stations are scattered across Andalusia, connecting cities with picturesque countryside destinations.

Major cities like Seville, Granada, and Malaga have central train stations where you can catch regional trains.

Ticket Costs: Regional train tickets for short distances range from €5 to €15, depending on the destination. Booking in advance or using regional passes can often secure better rates.

Opting for Intercity Buses:

Finding Bus Terminals: Intercity buses are an economical choice for exploring the Andalusian countryside. Locate bus terminals in major cities, such as Seville's Plaza de Armas or Malaga's Estación de Autobuses.

Budget-Friendly Fares: Intercity bus fares vary based on distance, but you can expect to pay approximately €10 to €25 for longer journeys. Researching routes and schedules in advance allows you to plan your countryside exploration more efficiently.

Embracing Local Transportation Hubs:

Rural Bus Stations: In smaller towns and villages, local bus stations connect with regional hubs. Embrace the charm of rural transportation, ensuring you get a genuine taste of Andalusian life.

Affordable Transfers: Local buses in rural areas often have lower fares, ranging from €1 to €5 for short trips. Connecting to regional hubs enables you to explore the countryside at a fraction of the cost.
Considering Carpooling and Ridesharing:

Online Platforms: Explore ridesharing and carpooling platforms, where locals offer shared rides to and from rural destinations. Websites and apps facilitate connections, providing an affordable and sociable means of transportation.

Contribution Models: Costs for ridesharing can vary, but contributing €5 to €15 for a shared ride is common.

This not only reduces expenses but also offers a chance to meet locals and fellow travelers.

Navigating Andalusia affordably involves a combination of cost-effective urban transportation and strategic exploration of the countryside. By tapping into regional trains, intercity buses, local transportation hubs, and innovative ridesharing options, you can immerse yourself in the diverse landscapes and vibrant culture of Andalusia without exceeding your travel budget.

Immersing in Local Culture

Andalusia is not merely a destination; it's a cultural Fabric woven with spontaneity, lively street life, and budget-friendly nocturnal experiences. Dive into the heart of local culture as you participate in spontaneous events, soak in the atmosphere of bustling streets, and discover nightlife gems that won't dent your wallet.

1. Participating in Spontaneous Cultural Events:

Uncovering Local Festivals:

Local Calendars: Tap into the cultural pulse of Andalusia by checking local event calendars. Many towns and cities host spontaneous festivals celebrating everything from music and dance to food and folklore.

Free Events: Keep an eye out for free cultural events, such as street performances, parades, and outdoor concerts. These impromptu gatherings provide an authentic glimpse into Andalusia's rich cultural heritage.

Street Art and Performances:

Exploring Artistic Hubs: Wander through neighborhoods adorned with street art and murals. Cities like Seville and Granada boast vibrant artistic communities, often expressing their creativity in public spaces.

Street Performances: From flamenco guitarists to spontaneous dance performances, the streets of Andalusia come alive with artistic expression. Join the audience and let the rhythm of the streets become your guide to local culture.

2. Soaking in the Atmosphere of Lively Street Life:

Exploring Local Markets:

Mercados: Immerse yourself in the lively atmosphere of local markets, or mercados, where vendors showcase fresh produce, handmade crafts, and regional delicacies. These bustling markets are not only sensory delights but also budget-friendly spaces to experience daily life.

Interacting with Vendors: Strike up conversations with vendors, inquire about local products, and embrace the camaraderie of the market. Engaging with the locals in these vibrant spaces offers a genuine connection to Andalusian street life.

Plazas and Public Spaces:

Central Plazas: The heart of Andalusian cities lies in their central plazas. Whether it's Seville's Plaza de España oro Granada's Plaza Nueva, these public spaces host a spectrum of activities, from live music to cultural events.

Café Culture: Find a seat at a café overlooking a bustling plaza, order a coffee or a glass of local wine, and witness the ebb and flow of daily life. This leisurely approach to street life allows you to absorb the rhythms of Andalusian culture.

3. Budget-Friendly Nightlife Experiences:

Tavernas and Bodegas:

Traditional Taverns: Dive into the local nightlife by visiting traditional taverns and bodegas. These intimate venues often offer live music, and some even host spontaneous jam sessions. Enjoy a glass of wine or a local beer while absorbing the authentic sounds of Andalusian music.

Happy Hour Specials: Take advantage of happy hour specials, which are common in many bars. This budget-friendly timeframe allows you to enjoy the ambiance and social scene without overspending.

Flamenco in Peñas:

Peñas Flamencas: For an authentic flamenco experience without the high costs of commercial shows, seek out peñas flamencas—intimate venues where local artists gather. These gatherings provide a raw and heartfelt expression of flamenco, allowing you to connect with this iconic Andalusian art form on a budget.
Beachside Chiringuitos:

Chiringuitos: If you find yourself along the Costa del Sol, explore the beachside Chiringuitos. These open-air bars often feature live music and a relaxed atmosphere. Grab a seat by the shore, enjoy a refreshing cocktail, and let the Mediterranean breeze accompany your budget-friendly beachside evening.

Conclusion

As the sun sets over the rugged landscapes of Andalucía and the Costa del Sol, it casts a warm glow on the memories of a journey that seamlessly blended beauty and affordability. The allure of this southern Spanish region lies not just in its historic cities, charming villages, or pristine beaches but also in the accessibility of its wonders for budget-conscious travelers.

Reflecting on the Beauty and Affordability:

Andalucía, with its Moorish wonders, lively street life, and flavorful cuisine, unveils an array of experiences that transcends the boundaries of cost. From the majestic Alhambra to the intimate taverns of Seville, every corner resonates with the rich cultural heritage of the region. The affordability of transportation, the charm of budget-friendly local eateries, and the spontaneity of cultural events create a mosaic of memories that prove that exploring the beauty of Andalucía doesn't require a lavish budget.

The Costa del Sol, adorned with seaside villages and hidden gems, invites travelers to unwind along its sun-kissed shores without straining their wallets. From the tranquil beaches of Nerja to the vibrant promenades of Estepona, the coastal experience is not just a feast for the senses but also a testament to the affordability of seaside adventures.

Encouraging Budget Travelers to Explore:

To fellow budget travelers seeking a blend of cultural richness and economic sensibility, Andalucía and the Costa del Sol extend an open invitation. Whether you're wandering through the historic streets of Granada, savoring tapas in a local tavern, or discovering hidden gems along the coast, each moment becomes a testament to the accessibility of this captivating region.

Andalucía, with its blend of history, culture, and warmth, welcomes budget-conscious explorers with open arms. The affordability of accommodations, the efficiency of public transportation, and the charm of budget-friendly local eateries make it not just a feasible destination but an enriching one.

In the rhythm of flamenco, the flavors of Andalusian cuisine, and the warmth of its people, budget travelers find a haven where their curiosity can flourish without financial constraints. Andalucía and the Costa del Sol beckon with a promise—an assurance that the journey will be as enriching to the soul as it is gentle on the pocket.

So, to those with an adventurous spirit and a mindful budget, set your compass towards Andalucía and the Costa del Sol.

Unveil the beauty that lies in the convergence of affordability and splendor, and let the echoes of this journey resonate as an ode to the magic that can be woven when exploration meets economic sensibility.

Printed in Great Britain
by Amazon

36312337R00046